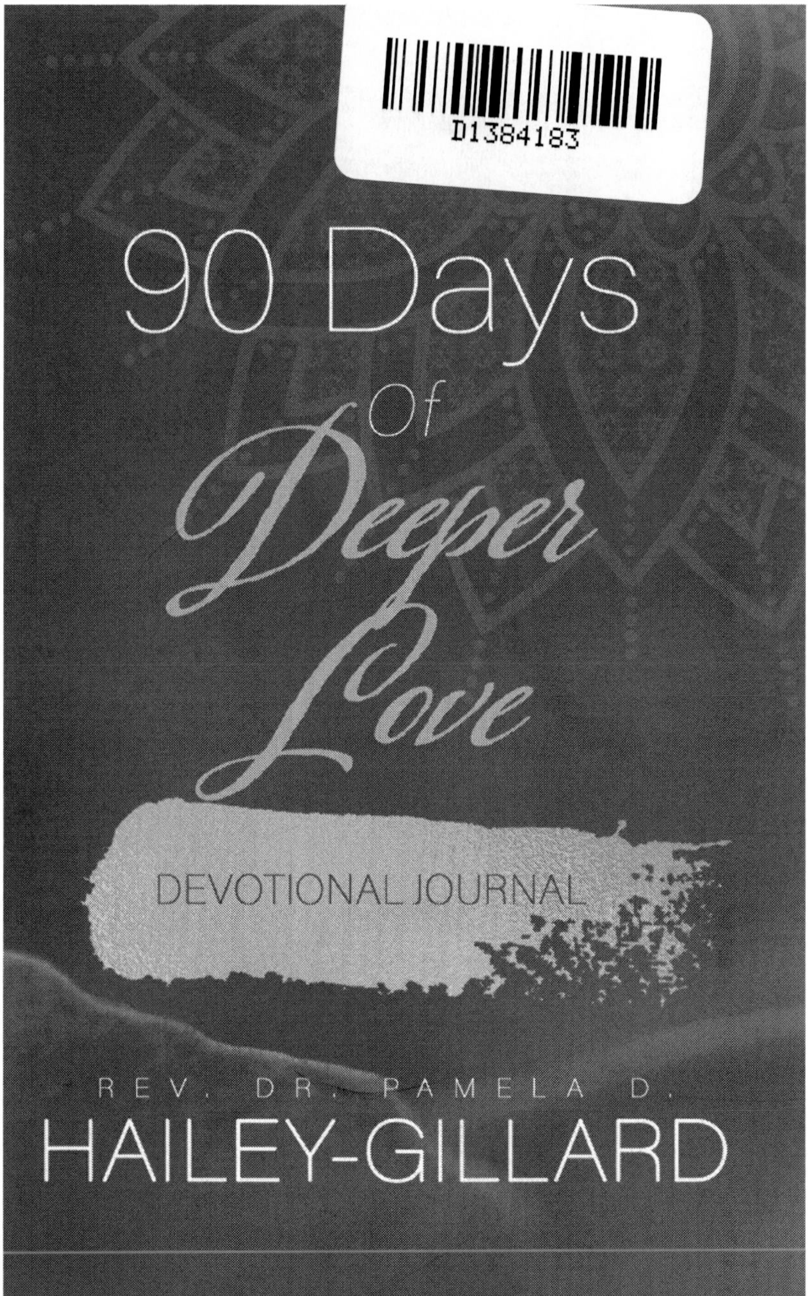

Extreme Overflow Publishing
Dacula, GA
USA

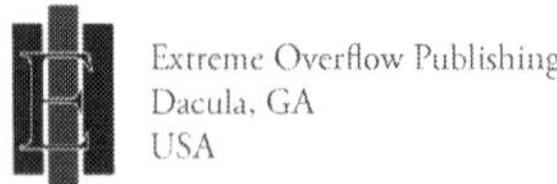

Extreme Overflow Publishing

A Brand of Extreme Overflow Enterprises, Inc

P.O. Box 1811

Dacula, GA 30019

www.extremeoverflow.com

Send feedback to info@extremeoverflow.com

Printed in the United States of America

Library of Congress Catalogin-Publication

Data is available for this title. ISBN: 978-1-7379262-4-5

90 Days of Deeper Love

DEVOTIONAL JOURNAL

REV. DR. PAMELA D. HAILEY-GILLARD

To:

From:

Date:

From the Author

As chaotic as things may seem, we are still alive Praise the Lord for another day. Can I get a witness? My dream of completing this work has finally become a reality. I have been inspired by some of the greatest men and women of all times and want to thank them publicly.

My husband of 29 years, Daniel, the love of my life, my best friend, I thank you for your support.

Jamil, my heartbeat, Reebee and Danny

my gifts from God, Cianna, Jamil Jr., Devin, T'yanna, Payton, Niyah, and Damir my seed, Jeannine, Daniel and Jahzeel my jewels, you have all brought much joy to my life.

Jimmy, Paula, Cherry, Ricky, Barbara, Stevie, (Dennis, Tunnie, Chucky, Lynne, Warren, LeRoy all deceased) Brothers and Sisters for life. To all my Spiritual Sons and Daughters, my added Blessings, I love and treasure all of you.

My mother Mildred C. (Younger) Hailey, my dad, Jimmy Hailey, Grandmother Mary Mildred Younger, Great-grandmother, Cora L. Moody, Uncle James and My Aunts Peggy, Tommie and Cynthia; Rev. Leanna Jones, Pastors, Dwayne Johnson, and Deborah Johnson, I honor you and my (Bromley-Heath and New Orleans) village.

Special thanks to my Pastors, Bishop John M. Borders, III and First Lady Sandra E. Borders, Rev. Dorothy Isles-Smith, Pastors Ray &

Janet Taranto, Rev. Ernest London (deceased) and 1st Lady Marie who have inspired and encouraged me.

These devotionals were birthed during major events in my life and gave me strength and courage to face each day through the Word of God and Prayer. It is my hope that you will draw from this well what you need, when you need it and use it to go deeper as you reflect on God's love.

Love and Blessings,

Rev Dr Pamela Hailey-Gillard

Devotional Journal

Day 1

Renewed Mind

Daily we are bombarded by the media, outside influences and opinions of men. Our minds can be overwhelmed with a variety of things and cause us to do and say things that take us from the Word of God. Take a few moments to get before God and he will transform and renew your mind through the Word of God.

> Let this mind be in you. which was also in christ Jesus.
>
> **Philippians 2:5**

Today's Prayer

Lord I pray that your steady hand would guide me. I pray for my family, community, church and I pray for your mighty hand to move.

I pray for a renewal of heart and mind. Touch me in the way I need it the most. Remove all fear and doubt. Continue to heal those who are suffering from illnesses. Continue to comfort those who suffer losses of loved ones and heal their grieving hearts. I thank God for the Blood of Jesus that covers me, my family, friends and all who call upon Him.

Lord breathe on us all!

Amen.

I decree and declare that

my mind is renewed and

I will fulfill God's will in my life.

DAY 1

1. **How has renewing your mind been a struggle for you?**

____

____

____

____

2. **What might God be trying to teach you in the process?**

____

____

____

____

Day 2

Trusting God To See You Through

As believers we trust the Word of God to see us through. When we feel overwhelmed, and anxious because of what we hear, see, or feel, we must look to God for strength, peace and faith.

> Trust in the Lord with all your heart and lean not on your own understanding. In all your ways acknowledge Him, and He will make your paths straight.
>
> **Proverbs 3:5-6**

Today's Prayer

I pray Lord, that you teach me how to trust you. Help me to not allow the past hurts and pain to keep me from believing and receiving from you. I am trusting you as my testimony is being built and my faith increases. I trust you with my life and the lives of those I love.

Amen.

I decree and declare that

I will trust you with my whole heart and

acknowledge that you are at work in my life.

Day 2

1. How has trusting God to see you through been a struggle for you?

____

____

____

____

2. What might God be trying to teach you in the process?

____

____

____

____

Day 3

Receiving Comfort

Whatever you receive is not just for you. It is to be passed on in a time of need. We serve a God who cares about everything we go through.

> Praise be to the God and Father of our Lord Jesus Christ, the Father of Compassion and the God of all comfort who comforts us in all our troubles, so that we can comfort those in any trouble with the comfort we ourselves receive from God.
>
> **2 Corinthians 1:3-4**

Today's Prayer

I pray for comfort in all that I am going through spiritually, physically and mentally. As I am comforted, I will offer that comfort to someone else who is feeling pain in their situation.

Amen.

I decree and declare that
God is comforting me on my journey
and I will comfort my brother and sister
with the same comfort.

Day 3

1. How has receiving comfort been a struggle for you?

____

____

____

____

2. What might God be trying to teach you in the process?

____

____

____

____

Day 4

Pressing On

As you press your way through life and the situations that we find ourselves confronted with, don't give up. You have not come this far to give up now. Don't give up on your child. Don't give up on your marriage. Don't give up on what God says is for YOU. Exercise a little more patience so you can endure. Your victory is right over the hill, can you see it? God has not brought you this far to leave you. Press on. It will be worth it!

> Let I press on toward the goal for the prize of the upward call of God in Christ Jesus.

Philipians 3:14

Today's Prayer

I pray for courage and strength to believe God and to endure the process. I pray when things get difficult, I will keep going. Help me to keep pressing because when I do, I will have the victory in Christ Jesus. I thank you God that I am entering a new season and I know the best is yet to come.

Amen.

I decree and declare that

I will not give up,

I am going all the way with the Lord.

Day 4

1. How has pressing on been a struggle for you?

____

____

____

____

2. What might God be trying to teach you in the process?

____

____

____

____

Day 5

Keeping A Consistent Flow

Keep a consistency flowing in your heart. Keep it clean. It is easy during difficult times to be angry, bitter, mean spirited and unforgiving because of things that happen to us. Daily we must ask God for forgiveness of our sins and forgive others who have sinned against us. Also, we must learn to forgive ourselves because once we give it to the Lord, we need not carry it's burden any longer.

> Above all else, guard your heart, for everything you do flows from it.
>
> **Proverbs 4:23**

Today's Prayer

I pray for those who have wronged me, and those I have wronged. I ask God to heal us and forgive us. I pray that I walk in the light of Jesus with a pure heart turned to you. Thank you for miracles, breakthroughs, and sudden blessings.

Amen.

I decree and declare that
a consistent flow of God's love,
peace and joy are flowing from my heart.

Day 5

1. How has keeping a consistent flow in your heart been a struggle for you?

____

____

____

____

2. What might God be trying to teach you in the process?

____

____

____

____

Day 6

Believe

I know that sometimes in our faith we can readily believe for others but when it comes to ourselves, we have a tendency to waiver. Begin to rejoice like you have already received what you have prayed for.

> Truly, I tell you, if anyone says to this mountain, “go throw yourself into the sea;” and does not doubt in their heart but believes that what they say will happen, it will be done for them. Therefore, I tell you, whatever you ask for in prayer, believe that you have received it, and it will be yours.

Mark 11:23-24

Today's Prayer

I pray for signs, miracles and wonders to follow me and my family because I believe. I pray for the manifestation of God's word to eradicate all doubt. I thank and pray for mountain moving experiences to change me on my journey.

Amen.

I decree and declare that

as I pray, the mountains will

melt like wax.

Day 6

1. How has believing God's Word been a struggle for you?

____

____

____

____

2. What might God be trying to teach you in the process?

____

____

____

____

Day 7

Perseverance

It seems like the trials and tribulations in our lives are never ending. If you come out of one thing, before you catch your breath you are going through another. We can look at another perspective - we are made strong through our weaknesses. They are designed to grow us up. Your trial has a purpose in your life. Count it all joy.

> Consider it pure joy, my brothers and sisters, whenever you face trials of many kinds, because you know the testing of your faith produces perseverance. Let perseverance finish its work so that you may be mature and complete, not lacking anything.

James 1:2-4

Today's Prayer

I pray for clarity in this trial and that I will come out of this trial knowing that you are a healer, deliverer and a restorer. I will not murmur or complain but I will praise my way through. I pray for miracles and supernatural turnaround and favor to follow me and all the courageous followers of Christ. I will in Jesus's Name pass this test.

Amen.

I decree and declare that
my trials will not break me but will
help make me to be stronger in my walk.

Day 7

1. **How has perseverance been a struggle for you?**

____

____

____

____

2. **What might God be trying to teach you in the process?**

____

____

____

____

Day 8

Waiting

Waiting is difficult for most of us because we want it now. Waiting also requires that we trust and have faith in the one that we are waiting for, the situation that we need to be resolved or the service we need to be provided, the mate that we want, the list goes on.

What is your attitude like while you are waiting? Are you short on patience? Or are you kind and pleasant to others? Go to the source - Jesus Christ. Wait upon the Lord.

> Be still before the Lord and wait patiently for him; fret not yourself over the one who prospers in His way, over the man who carries out evil devices!
>
> **Psalm 37:7**

Today's Prayer

Lord I ask for your guidance as I wait upon you. Help me to be patient, help me to be kind and patient as I wait. I pray for a guard over my heart that I will not murmur or complain. I pray for a change in our leadership, I pray that I will realize that whatever you have for me and my family is worth waiting for.

Amen.

I decree and declare that

I have a new attitude as I wait.

Day 8

1. How has waiting been a struggle for you?

____

____

____

____

2. What might God be trying to teach you in the process?

____

____

____

____

Day 9

Clean Slate

At some point in our lives, we have all been guilty of making a mistake. Some mistakes we can correct with an eraser or the stroke of a pen, others we are faced with and still are facing. When we come into the knowledge of Jesus Christ and we ask Him to forgive us of our sins, He wipes our slates clean. However, we still are presented with consequences for our actions, but guess what they still work together for our good and the good of others.

> Keep your servant also from willful sins;
> may they not rule over me. Then I will be
> blameless, innocent of great transgression.

Psalm 19:13

Today's Prayer

I pray that we receive the power of the Holy Spirit in our lives that can heal us deliver us and change us. I pray for a heart of repentance. Help us Lord to be Christlike in our families and communities. Thank you for the Blood of Jesus that covers, protects and cleanses me.

Amen.

I decree and declare that
God has wiped my slate clean
and given me a brand-new start.

Day 9

1. **How has wiping the slate clean been a struggle for you?**

____

____

____

____

2. **What might God be trying to teach you in the process?**

____

____

____

____

Day 10

Communication

Prayer changes things. Do we have a consistent prayer life or is it on a 911 basis? Prayer is communication with God. When is the last time you had a heart to heart with the Lord? He wants to hear from you. Also, the Bible lets us know that we need to fast along with our praying.

It's time to turn back to God. We are waiting on Him, but He is waiting on us. I pray for a turnaround in our hearts today.

> But when you pray, go into your room, close the door and pray to your Father, who is unseen. Then your Father who sees what is done in secret, will reward you.
>
> **Matthew 6:6**

Today's Prayer

I pray Lord that you would hear me when I call out to you. I ask that you would teach me how to pray and grant me the petitions that I stand in need of. I want to be consistent in my prayer life and I ask for guidance in this area in Jesus' name.

Amen.

I decree and declare that
my secret time with my Father
will bring great rewards.

DAY 10

1. How has communication with God through prayer been a struggle for you?

____

____

____

____

2. What might God be trying to teach you in the process?

____

____

____

____

Devotional Journal

Day 11

Praise

Can you praise your way through your anger, your disappointments, frustrations and sufferings? You can bring all of your stuff to the Lord because He can handle it. He will give you rest as you praise your way through.

> From the rising of the sun unto the going down
> of the same the Lord's Name is to be praised.
>
> **Psalm 113:3**

Today's Prayer

I pray and give my burdens to you. Heal my heart so that I may praise you with a grateful heart. I give you praise because you are a Mighty good God even when I am going through.

Amen.

I decree and declare that
I will praise my way through
the good and bad times.

DAY 11

1. How has your praise to God through prayer been a struggle for you?

____

____

____

____

2. What might God be trying to teach you in the process?

____

____

____

____

Day 12

A New Thing

God is doing a new and great thing in the midst of us. You are currently walking in your new normal. The unknown can tempt or cause you to turn back to what you knew or what was familiar. Instead, be sensitive to what God says in this new season. As you listen, you may notice some things were broken that needed to be.

He is my way maker, my miracle worker, my promise keeper, my light in my darkness, that is who God is.

> Behold I will do a new thing; now it shall spring forth, and ye shall not know it. I will even make a way in the wilderness, and rivers in the desert.
>
> **Isaiah 43:19**

Today's Prayer

I pray for an outpouring of God's spirit. I await my new season, my new thing that you are doing in my life. I thank you for renewing my mind and spirit that I may receive what you have for me. I pray in thanksgiving for what is about to spring forth.

Amen.

I decree and declare that

I have a new season

springing forth in my life.

Day 12

1. How has your new season with God through prayer been a struggle for you?

____

____

____

____

2. What might God be trying to teach you in the process?

____

____

____

____

Day 13

Stand

Keep on Standing. God has you in his hands. We can stand on God's Word and what He said He will bring to pass.

> Therefore, put on the full armor of God, so that when the day of evil comes, you may be able to stand your ground, and after you have done everything, to stand.

Ephesians 6:13

—

Today's Prayer

I pray for exposure to everything that is hidden within me. Everything that weakens my stand for you. I pray for Miracles, signs and wonders to manifest as I stand taller for you.

Amen.

I decree and declare that

I will stand in the midst of adversity.

DAY 13

1. How has your stance with God through prayer been a struggle for you?

____

____

____

____

2. What might God be trying to teach you in the process?

____

____

____

____

Day 14

Promises

The promises of God are obtainable. God has a plan and a purpose for you and He will bring it to pass. How bad do you want to see them? Press your way to what God has for you in this season.

> For no matter how many promises God has made, they are "Yes" in Christ. And so through him the "Amen" is spoken by us to the glory of God.
>
> **2 Corinthians 1:20**

—

Today's Prayer

I pray that God would release his promises where we need to be revived in our belief the most. I pray for an outpouring of miracles, break-throughs, and releasing of oppression and depression so I may see your promise manifested.

Amen.

I decree and declare that
God is a promise keeper and I will
see these promises come to pass.

Day 14

1. How has seeing or not seeing the promises of God in your life through been a struggle for you?

____

____

____

____

2. What might God be trying to teach you in the process?

____

____

____

____

Day 15

All for Good

Don't worry when trials and tribulations seem to follow you. Know that it is going to work something far more precious than you can imagine.

You see, what others may have planned as evil against you, God will use for your good.

> And we know that in all things God works for the good of those who love him, who have been called according to his purpose.

Romans 8:28

Today's Prayer

I pray for courage to forgive anyone that has harmed me physically or intentionally harmed my character. I thank God for turning what they meant for harm, for my good. I pray for healing of my mind, body, and spirit. I pray for wisdom and confidence to endure because you are with me.

Amen.

I decree and declare that

God is working on my behalf.

DAY 15

1. How has unforgiveness been a struggle for you?

____

____

____

____

2. What might God be trying to teach you in the process?

____

____

____

____

Day 16

Count it All Joy

We tend to forget what God has done in our lives and what He has brought us through and how He will do it again. It is good to just pause, reflect and thank the Lord for making a way, keeping you from all seen and unseen danger, healing your body, protecting you, and the list of many blessings goes on.

We can count it all joy because He will sustain us. He will never suffer the righteous to be moved.

> My lips will shout for joy when I sing praise to You - I whom you have delivered.
>
> **Psalm 71:23**

Today's Prayer

I pray for an outpouring of God's Spirit to fall upon us, to lead, guide and direct us into all truth. I thank you for bringing me through my trials, I will serve you with joy.

Amen.

I decree and declare that

my joy gives me strength and

will sustain me.

Day 16

1. How has your appreciation to God through prayer been a struggle for you?

____

____

____

____

2. What might God be trying to teach you in the process?

____

____

____

____

Day 17

Faint Not

It's time to get excited about all the possibilities that God has in store for you. This is a time like no other in our lives that require faith, obedience and patience and we will reap if we faint not.

We must continue, we must press, we can't get tired now. Others are depending on your journey, on your testimony. Just hit the reset button and be refreshed.

Don't Give Up!

> Let us not become weary in doing good, for at the proper time we will reap a harvest if we do not give up.
>
> **Galatians 6:9-10**

Today's Prayer

I pray for an outpouring of the Holy Spirit to refresh, revive and renew my prospective. I ask for a repentant heart that turns to the Lord. I pray for fortitude and peace. Forever will I praise the name of the Lord.

Amen.

I decree and declare that
I will not give up when I am weary
because you are with me.

DAY 17

1. How has your strength been a struggle for you?

---

2. What might God be trying to teach you in the process?

Day 18

Trust

If you have ever been disappointed or let down by a friend, a spouse or a relative, it can be a crippling experience causing you to have trust issues in other relationships. The good news is, God wants to restore and repair the damage broken relationships has caused you. When you put your trust in God you will never be disappointed. You can trust God with all of your heart. Systems fail, plans fail, man will fail but God never fails.

In order to fully embrace what God wants to do through you, you must learn how to let go of the past hurt and start trusting in Him. He is able but you must be willing.

When I am afraid, I put my trust in you.

Psalm 56:3

Today's Prayer

I pray today for total complete healing of my heart, body and soul. Today, I let go of past hurts and make room for a new trust-filled relationship with You God. Let the Spirit of the Living God fall fresh upon on me and fill me to overflowing capacity.

Amen.

I decree and declare that

I can and will trust God with my life.

Day 18

1. How has your trust in God through prayer been a struggle for you?

____

____

____

____

2. What might God be trying to teach you in the process?

____

____

____

____

Day 19

Committment

It is our responsibility to act on what we hear. When we hear God's voice, the action that follows categorizes our commitment as being a hearer or a doer that God can depend upon to do what needs to be done on earth to glorify his name. Which are you?

> But be doers of the Word, and not hearers only, deceiving yourselves.
>
> **James 1:22**

Today's Prayer

I pray that I will hear and do what you say. I will be led by the voice of God and I will stay true to the course.

Amen.

I decree and declare that

I will honor my commitment to God

and do what He says to do.

DAY 19

1. How has you being a doer of God's word through prayer been a struggle for you?

____

____

____

____

2. What might God be trying to teach you in the process?

____

____

____

____

Devotional Journal

Day 20

No Distractions

At God's appointed time, He will move. God has a plan that He will execute in the earth through you. Don't allow the enemy to distract you with this and that.

This means, we must stay focused and allow God to show us great and mighty things. God does not want us to be caught up in foolish distractions.

> No one serving as a soldier gets entangled in civilian affairs, but rather tries to please his commanding officer.
>
> **2 Timothy 2:4**

Today's Prayer

I pray that I will not be distracted from my path. I pray for discernment and exposure where they are present and I can use wisdom to avoid. Lord be merciful to us. Continue to keep us preserved and reserved for your will.

Amen.

I decree and declare that

if I become distracted I will

redirect my focus.

Day 20

1. How has your communication with God through prayer been a struggle for you?

____

____

____

____

2. What might God be trying to teach you in the process?

____

____

____

____

Day 21

One Voice

We must be very selective in whom we allow in our gates (eyes, ears) and what we set our sight on. So, when it comes to relationships, businesses, and ministry you will need the discernment of the Holy Spirit. Otherwise, where there are too many voices, there will be too many reports.

> My sheep listen to my voice; I know them, and they follow me.
>
> **John 10:27**

Today's Prayer

I pray to hear your voice better. Incline my ear to Your heart that my discernment would be sharpened to know Your voice over the many others in my life.

Amen.

I decree and declare that

I hear and know God's voice and I will follow.

Day 21

1. How has your ear toward God through prayer been a struggle for you?

____

____

____

____

2. What might God be trying to teach you in the process?

____

____

____

____

Day 22

Flames

How hot are the flames in your life? Sometimes the flames of life, those small issues we can't put out, get hot, even very hot. He will be there with you in the fire, in the flames. You are never alone.

The flames of purifying fire come to refine our gifts, attitudes, mindsets, and gifts. When we come forth from the fiery flames, we will be stronger and shine bright as pure gold. The hotter the flame the greater His Presence.

> When you pass through the waters, I will be with you; and when you pass through the rivers, they will not sweep over you. When you walk through the fire, you will not be burned; the flames will not set you ablaze.
>
> **Isaiah 43:2**

Today's Prayer

I pray for the power and the anointing of the Holy Spirit to set our soul ablaze. May it break every chain and deliver us from the hand of the enemy. I pray that you would move us away from any fear because you hold us. Thank you for walking with me through the fire.

Amen.

I decree and declare that

the fires of life will not engulf me

because God is with me.

Day 22

1. How have the fiery flames of life been a struggle for you?

____

____

____

____

2. What might God be trying to teach you in the process?

____

____

____

____

Day 23

Attitude

You can put on a brand-new attitude like a brand-new shirt. Press the delete button on everything that was negative, unfruitful, hurtful, painful, shameful. Release those thoughts and attitudes that are aligned contrary to the Word of God. How do you change your attitude?

Reboot your mind with positive affirmations, build up and edify yourself, getting ready for beautiful change occurring through God's manifested power.

> Therefore, if any man be in Christ, he is a new creature; old things are passed away; behold, all things are become new.
>
> **2 Corinthians 5:17**

Today's Prayer

I pray for the power of the Holy Spirit to fall on me, right now. In a fresh release, deliver and set us free from every thought, emotion, idea and relationship that doesn't align with your will.

Amen.

I decree and declare that

I am going higher in God.

Day 23

1. How has your attitude with God through prayer been a struggle for you?

____

____

____

____

2. What might God be trying to teach you in the process?

____

____

____

____

Day 24

Face Forward

God wants to do great things in you and for you. But you have to keep moving forward. Don't stop. Only look back to see how far you have come. Let your eyes look directly forward, and your gaze be straight before you.

> Let your eyes look straight ahead, fix your gaze directly before you.
>
> **Proverbs 4:25**

Today's Prayer

I pray for the Spirit of truth to abide in me and help me to make wise decisions always focused on your present gift of life.

Amen.

I decree and declare that

I am moving forward

and I will not look back.

Day 24

1. How has your focus forward with God through prayer been a struggle for you?

____

____

____

____

2. What might God be trying to teach you in the process?

____

____

____

____

Day 25

The Best

You may have heard it before. The truth still remains. The best, God's best, is yet to come in your life. No matter what you are going through, things will get better.

> But as it is written, what no eye has seen, no ear has heard, and no human heart has conceived - God has prepared these things for those who love him.
>
> **1 Corinthians 2:9**

Today's Prayer

I pray for the peace of God to overshadow me and fill my heart with the peace of knowing you always have my best interest in mind.

Amen.

I decree and declare that

my best days are ahead of me.

Day 25

1. How has you knowing God's best is coming been a struggle for you?

____

____

____

____

2. What might God be trying to teach you in the process?

____

____

____

____

Day 26

Forgiveness

One of the hardest things to do sometimes is to admit that we are wrong or we made a mistake. Pride will not allow us to say I am sorry. Then we wonder why our blessings are hindered. Humility clears the path for blessings.

Now you might feel, “I can’t forgive - you don’t know what they did!” Jesus tells us plain and simple. For if you forgive other people when they sin against you, your Heavenly Father will also forgive you. Be encouraged. If you struggle in this area, ask God to help you. Sooner than later, we will need God to forgive us for something, so let us get ready to walk in a new freedom.

> Bear with each other and forgive one another if any of you has a grievance against someone. Forgive as the Lord forgave you.
>
> **Colossians 3:13**

Today's Prayer

I humble my heart before you and ask that you forgive me of my sins. I pray that I will forgive others as you have forgiven me. Help me to not hold grudges and to release others as you have released me.

Amen.

I decree and declare that

I will no longer hold anyone hostage.

You are forgiven.

Day 26

1. How has your forgiveness level been a struggle for you?

____

____

____

____

2. What might God be trying to teach you in the process?

____

____

____

____

Day 27

Speak

What are you speaking? Are you speaking words of life or words of death? Words of faith or fear? Are your words edifying or do they tear people down? Speak positivity instead of negativity. Let your speech be reflective of the Word of God. Watch what you speak over yourself, your family and others.

I am reminded through the Word of God what you say can preserve life or destroy, so you must accept the consequences of your words

> Death and life are in the power of the tongue,
> and those who love it will eat its fruits.
>
> **Proverbs 18:21**

—

Today's Prayer

I pray for the confidence to speak positively. I pray for the heart to speak sweet words to everyone I meet. Help me to see with your view in mind. Send compassion to fill my heart and I will be careful to praise you in advance.

Amen.

I decree and declare that

I speak well over myself and others.

Day 27

1. How has your communication with others been a struggle for you?

____

____

____

____

2. What might God be trying to teach you in the process?

____

____

____

____

Day 28

New Grace

We are expected to live an ongoing life of repentance, so why are we allowing the enemy to torment us with past mistakes and failures of things we did and did not do? God does not remember them and neither should you.

You can begin again.

> Though your beginning was insignificant, yet your end will increase gently.
>
> **Job 8:7**

Today's Prayer

I pray to see myself through the eyes of Christ. I forgive myself of the past and commit to keeping it moving. I pray for healing to be manifested in my life. I pray that every tormenting spirit on assignment to plague me be sent far away from me. I pray for supernatural power to move all around me.

Amen.

I decree and declare that

I am who God says I am.

Day 28

1. How has accepting grace for your past mistakes and moving forward from the past been a struggle for you?

____

____

____

____

2. What might God be trying to teach you in the process?

____

____

____

____

Day 29

Keep on Praying

You do not need permission. You do not need a degree or credentials. All you need is a heart to pray. Instead of talking about something why not pray about it? God wants to hear from you. Standing, sitting, kneeling, or stretched out in His presence is all He wants.

> Pray without ceasing
>
> **1 Thessalonians 5:17**

Today's Prayer

I ask for an outpouring of your Spirit today for healing in my body, in my home, in my community and our country. I pray for supernatural turnaround for everything around me that is contrary to your will. I pray for miracles and signs and wonders to follow me and everyone I am connected to.

Amen.

I decree and declare that

I will stand in prayer.

Day 29

1. How has praying for yourself and others been a struggle for you?

____

____

____

____

2. What might God be trying to teach you in the process?

____

____

____

____

Day 30

Created for Good

When was the last time you did something good for someone else? As you approach each day, meet it as an assignment from God to think of others with a corresponding action. This is confirmation that you can do it. Whatever God entrusts to you to do, just do it and give your best.

> For we are His workmanship, created in Christ Jesus for good works, which God prepared beforehand, that we should walk in them.
>
> **Ephesians 2:10**

Today's Prayer

I pray and thank God that I am a work in progress and I am still under construction. God's hand is continually upon my life and my loved ones. I am made in the image of God and I ask that God will make me over until I look just like him. I thank God that He has created me for such a time as this.

Amen.

I decree and declare that

I am God's masterpiece.

Day 30

1. How has doing something good for someone else been a struggle for you?

____

____

____

____

2. What might God be trying to teach you in the process?

____

____

____

____

Devotional Journal

Day 31

Prayer Made Simple

Prayer is sometimes intimidating to people because they compare themselves to others, or feel they don't know how to pray. Prayer is really simple. It is spoken from your heart. It is amazing the benefits that prayer has to offer when you remove the pressure of how to pray. Prayer is powerful and can change any condition, give timely direction, prevent wrong decisions, eliminate anxiety and worry, produce peacefulness, protect us from discouragement, open doors of opportunity, and much more.

> We do not make requests because we are righteous but because of your great mercy.
>
> **Daniel 9:18**

Today's Prayer

I pray for renewal of relationships with God and others. I pray for an outpouring of the Holy Spirit today to heal, deliver and set free all who call on the Name of Jesus. I thank God for hearing and answering my prayers.

Amen.

I decree and declare that

my prayers are being answered.

Day 31

1. How has praying something good for someone else been a struggle for you?

____

____

____

____

2. What might God be trying to teach you in the process?

____

____

____

____

Day 32

Confidence

Be confident that God will answer you. He has no respect of person. Do you have confidence in God?

> And this is the confidence that we have toward him, that if we ask anything according to His will, He hears us. And if we know that He hears us in whatever we ask, we know that we have the requests that we have asked of Him.
>
> **1 John 5:14-15**

Today's Prayer

I pray that my confidence in God increases. I believe that God will do all that He says He will do. I pray for Miracles, Signs and Wonders to follow those who believe. I pray for great testimonies to be shared as we pray for our communities and our country. I know that there will be supernatural turn around as we pray for one another.

Amen.

I decree and declare that

my confidence is in God.

Day 32

1. How has confidence been a struggle for you?

____

____

____

____

2. What might God be trying to teach you in the process?

____

____

____

____

Day 33

Empowered

You have been empowered by Jesus the Christ to do great and mighty things and it all begins in prayer. Ask God what He has empowered you to do today. It can be as simple as a telephone call or a Prayer, or meeting a need in a sister or brother's life.

You have been given gifts not just for your benefit but for others. Prayer will give you insight and instruction on how to make this happen. I encourage you to just ask Lord, what will you have me to do?

> Ask, and it will be given to you, seek, and you will find, knock, and it will be opened to you.
>
> **Matthew 7:7**

Today's Prayer

I pray that I will stand on God's Word and know that I can do all things through Christ who strengthens me. I will and can do all the things that He has asked me to do and I know that He will do what I have asked of Him.

Amen.

I decree and declare that

I have what I ask of the Lord.

Day 33

1. How has personal empowerment been a struggle for you?

____

____

____

____

2. What might God be trying to teach you in the process?

____

____

____

____

Day 34

Devotion

I will devote myself to the things that pertain to God, the Kingdom, and the building of others. I will be mindful of what I do with my time. I pray for an awareness to my surroundings and I thank God for His loving kindness for me.

> This I say for your own benefit; not to put a restraint upon you, but to promote what is appropriate and to secure undistracted devotion to the Lord.
>
> Devote yourselves to prayer, being watchful and thankful. Open your mouth and tell it. Someone needs to hear of the goodness of God.

1 Corinthians 7:35

Today's Prayer

I pray for the power and the anointing of the Holy Spirit to touch our lives in the way we need it the most. Heal, deliver and set free all who are sick, oppressed, depressed and in need of the saving power of Jesus Christ. I pray for all who have battled any type of virus, and thank God for those who have recovered. I pray for broken hearts to be healed of those who have lost loved ones and are grieving. I pray for miracles, signs and wonders to follow all who believe.

Amen.

I decree and declare that

I am devoted to the Lord and His Word.

Day 34

1. How has devotion been a struggle for you?

____

____

____

____

2. What might God be trying to teach you in the process?

____

____

____

____

Day 35

Hope

So, we are not a people that walk around hopeless. God will see us through all of life's trials. Whatever you face today know that God is with you.

> Let us hold unswervingly to the hope we profess, for He who promised is faithful.
>
> **Hebrews 10:23**

Today's Prayer

I pray for the Anointing of the Holy Spirit to fall upon us; to heal us, revive us, and guide us. I pray that You would restore my hope as I speak the Word over my life. We pray for Miracles, Signs and Wonders to manifest. We bind and rebuke the spirits of fear, doubt, oppression, depression and low self-esteem. Violence and murder must go from our midst. Show us what to do. I pray that I will not be moved by what I see, but I will stand on God's Word which gives me hope. When I am in doubt, I will reflect on what God has done before.

Amen.

I decree and declare that

my hope is in the Lord.

Day 35

1. How has your hope level been a struggle for you?

____

____

____

____

2. What might God be trying to teach you in the process?

____

____

____

____

Day 36

Imitate

We go through life and sometimes we are not satisfied with ourselves, we want to be like this one or that one but if you want to imitate someone imitate Christ.

I want to encourage you to follow Christ's example. He left us instructions on how to walk out our salvation We must be imitators of Him to be successful. When we are faced with challenges that lead us in other directions or distract us from our purpose Jesus is right there to lead us back to Him. I want to encourage you today from the Scripture.

> Therefore, be imitators of God, as beloved children. And walk in love, as Christ loved us and gave himself up for us, a fragrant offering and sacrifice to God.
>
> **Ephesians 5:1-2**

Today's Prayer

I pray that I will become more Christlike day by day through prayer and the reading of God's Word. I will walk, talk, and look more like my Father through the power of the Holy Spirit.

Amen.

I decree and declare that

I want to walk like Christ walked on the earth.

Day 36

1. How has imitating God been a struggle for you?

____

____

____

____

2. What might God be trying to teach you in the process?

____

____

____

____

Day 37

Change

It's time to change your clothes. Take off doubt and fear and put on faith. Take off hate and discord and put on love. Take off weeping and put on joy. Bring your burdens to the Lord and leave them there. We are encouraged that they who mourn will be comforted.

> To appoint to those who mourn In Zion, to give them beauty for ashes, the oil of joy for mourning, the garment of praise for the spirit of heaviness; that they may be called trees of righteousness, the planting of the Lord that He might be glorified.
>
> **Isaiah 61:3**

Today's Prayer

I surrender every area of my life and ask for Your help in making the changes to bring You Honor Glory and Praise. I am changing everyday through the Word of God.

Amen.

I decree and declare that

I have my praise clothes on and

I will not take them off.

Day 37

1. How has change been a struggle for you?

____

____

____

____

2. What might God be trying to teach you in the process?

____

____

____

____

Day 38

Control

We all have areas in our lives where we feel that we have control, minimal control and have lost all control. Turn to the one who is always in Control, God our Father, and He will show you how to get it back.

> Listen to the advice and accept discipline, and at the end you will be counted among the wise. Many are the plans in a person's heart, but it is the Lord's purpose that prevails.
>
> **Proverbs 19:20-21**

Today's Prayer

I pray for God's plans for me to be revealed in my life. I will not resist the Holy Spirit to do the work in me.

Amen.

I decree and declare that
I want God to be in control of
all that concerns me.

Day 38

1. How has control been a struggle for you?

____

____

____

____

2. What might God be trying to teach you in the process?

____

____

____

____

Day 39

Truth

How do we know what is true or false? How do we know what is real or fake? Whose report shall we believe? I am going with God.

John 14:6, Jesus saith unto Him, I am the way, the truth, and the life; no man cometh unto the Father but by me.

> And ye shall know the truth, and the truth shall make you free.
>
> **John 8:32**

Today's Prayer

I pray for the Spirit of truth to lead, guide and direct me in the way I should go.

I pray for the Spirit of truth to reveal every plot and plan of the enemy. I pray for healing from every disease, signs and wonders to follow and a release of miracles this day.

Amen.

I decree and declare that

I am led by the Spirit of truth.

Day 39

1. How has truth been a struggle for you?

____

____

____

____

2. What might God be trying to teach you in the process?

____

____

____

____

Devotional Journal

Day 40

Clarity

Do you wonder sometimes about the many thoughts that plague your mind? I want to let you know that you do not have to receive these thoughts, these images of doubt, fear, what if, and negativity that the enemy brings our way. Torment of the past and the future have to go in the name of Jesus.

As soon as it hits your mind, get rid of it. See what the Word of God says and speak the Word over your situation.

> We demolish arguments and every pretension that sets itself up against the knowledge of God, and we take captive every thought to make it obedient to Christ.
>
> **2 Corinthians 10:5**

Today's Prayer

I pray for God to renew and restore my mind right now in the Name of Jesus through the power of the Holy Spirit. I pray for healing and deliverance for all who stand in need. I pray for those experiencing headaches, migraines, depression, chemical imbalances and torment in the mind. I believe that I will see clearly now.

Amen.

I decree and declare that
the Word of God will demolish every work
of the enemy.

Day 40

1. How has clarity been a struggle for you?

___

___

___

___

2. What might God be trying to teach you in the process?

___

___

___

___

Day 41

New Beginnings

God is birthing something new in your Spirit and there are things that must come to an end to walk in that newness of life. Do you sense it this morning? I want to encourage you today to be grateful, be thankful and realize that everyone does not have the promise of tomorrow. Love today, give today, enjoy today.

> Your beginnings will seem humble, so prosperous will your future be.
>
> **Job 8:7**

—

Today's Prayer

I pray that my mind has been renewed to begin new assignments, new tasks and new adventures and I am thankful for what lies ahead of me. I pray that I will walk humbly before God and men.

Amen.

I decree and declare that

God is doing something new in me.

Day 41

1. How have your new beginnings been a struggle for you?

____

____

____

____

2. What might God be trying to teach you in the process?

____

____

____

____

Day 42

First Choice

I can't imagine taking a step or making a decision without seeking God. We make time for things according to our personal priorities believing that we have time for the Lord's work; but something always seems to get away from us and it ends up on the to do list. Today I want to encourage you to make God and the things He asks us to do your first priority.

We will have a different outcome if He is our first choice instead of our last.

> Seek the Lord while He may be found, call on Him while He is near.
>
> **Isaiah 55:6**

Today's Prayer

I pray for the people of God to gather together and seek the Face of God like never before. I pray forgiveness of our sins and that we forgive each other.

Amen.

I decree and declare that

I choose to follow God and

I will seek Him first.

Day 42

1. How has first choice been a struggle for you?

____

____

____

____

2. What might God be trying to teach you in the process?

____

____

____

____

Day 43

See It

What do you see? Do you see just what's in front of you, your current situation or do you see in the future with eyes of the Spirit, beyond your circumstances?

> But as it is written, eye hath not seen, nor ear heard, neither have entered into the heart of man, the things which God hath prepared for them that love Him. But God hath revealed them unto us by His Spirit; for yea the Spirit searches all things, yea the deep things of God.
>
> **1 Corinthians 2:9-10**

Today's Prayer

I pray that my eyes are opened to the things that God would have me to see. I pray that I see beyond my current situation and I thank God for a glimpse of what is to come.

Amen.

I decree and declare that

I see through different lenses.

Day 43

1. **How has seeing it happen been a struggle for you?**

____

____

____

____

2. **What might God be trying to teach you in the process?**

____

____

____

____

Day 44

Thanksgiving

Give thanks! When we reflect over our lives, we can see what God has done, and it gives us confidence that He can do it again.

> All this is for your benefit, so that the grace that is reaching more and more people may cause thanksgiving to overflow to the glory of God. Therefore, we do not lose heart. Though outwardly we are wasting away, yet inwardly we are being renewed day by day.

2 Corinthians 4:15-16

Today's Prayer

Lord, thank you for healing and deliverance, thank you for sparing our lives and thank you for answered prayer. Thank you that you have been our provider. I appreciate all that God has done in my life and the lives of my loved ones.

Amen.

I decree and declare

my gratitude for all that God has done.

Day 44

1. How has gratitude been a struggle for you?

____

____

____

____

2. What might God be trying to teach you in the process?

____

____

____

____

Day 45

Hold On

God will see you through.

I want to encourage you to hold on. I know you have had some obstacles, some hindrances and unexpected things come your way, but you are going to make it.

> May the God of hope fill you with all joy and peace in believing, so that by the power of the Holy Spirit you may abound in hope.
>
> **Romans 15:13**

Today's Prayer

I pray for strength and endurance when I feel like letting go. I will hold on to the visions and the dreams, and stand firmly on the Word of God.

Amen.

I decree and declare that

God will never let me go.

Day 45

1. How has holding on been a struggle for you?

____

____

____

____

2. What might God be trying to teach you in the process?

____

____

____

____

Day 46

Right Now Blessings

I want to encourage you as you begin your day to expect God to move for you right now. Yesterday is gone, today is here and tomorrow awaits you.

> For I know the plans I have for you, declares the Lord, plans to prosper you and not to harm you, plans to give you hope and a future. Then you will call on me and come and pray to me, and I will listen to you. You will seek me and find me when you seek me with all of your heart.
>
> **Jeremiah 29:11-13**

Today's Prayer

I pray that you will give God your all. I believe God is moving on my behalf right now and I will see the manifestation.

Amen.

I decree and declare that

God has big plans for me.

Day 46

1. How has right now blessings been a struggle for you?

____

____

____

____

2. What might God be trying to teach you in the process?

____

____

____

____

Day 47

Focus

It is amazing how some prayers that we pray are answered before we can even give them to God and for others, we still are waiting for answers and manifestations.

Some situations will require turning off the tv and the phone, stepping back from social media, and turning over that plate and getting quiet before the Lord. Ask God for His direction as we make this our new normal. Let's get to it. How bad do you want it?

> But this kind does not go out but by fasting and prayer.
>
> **Matthew 17:21**

Today's Prayer

I pray for God to touch me in every area of my life. I pray for humble hearts and spirits. Lord when I am distracted help me to refocus on what is really important and what you have committed to my charge. I ask that you will help me to fast and pray from the things that try to entrap me.

Amen.

I decree and declare that

in Jesus's Name I will fast and pray and

see change in my situation.

Day 47

1. How has focus been a struggle for you?

____

____

____

____

2. What might God be trying to teach you in the process?

____

____

____

____

Day 48

Called for Purpose

You are called and have a purpose. God called you when you were in your mother's womb. He called you when you were in sin because he has something for you to do. He calls those who have been broken, hurn and in pain to carry out His purpose.

> But you are a chosen people, a royal priesthood, a holy nation, God's special posession, that you may declare the praises of him who called you out of darkness into his wonderful light.
>
> **1 Peter 2:9**

Today's Prayer

I pray for revelation knowledge of what my purpose is in this season and the courage to do what God says. I pray for healing power to touch and transform lives today. I pray for revelation of my purpose.

Thank you Lord, for your love poured upon me.

Amen.

I decree and declare that

I will walk in my purpose

as God reveals it to me.

Day 48

1. How has your calling been a struggle for you?

___

___

___

___

2. What might God be trying to teach you in the process?

___

___

___

___

Devotional Journal

Day 49

Victory is in the Air

During this season some of us have found ourselves full, doubtful, fearful, shameful, painful, and even sinful; just to name a few. We must begin to walk and talk as victorious over-comers. Some of us have never seen or experienced the things that we are now facing in our lifetime. We have murmured and complained, cussed and fussed, but God is here to deliver you. Victory is closer than you think. God is fighting for you!

> For the Lord your God is the one who goes with you to fight for you against your enemies to give you victory.
>
> **Deuteronomy 20:4**

Today's Prayer

I pray for victory over every situation in my life and I take authority over every spirit on assignment to hold me captive and defeat me. I thank God for setting me free from the things that have held me captive. I thank God for healing and deliverance in every area of my life and I know through the power of the Holy Spirit I will walk in victory.

Amen.

I decree and declare that
I am victorious through Christ Jesus
against my enemies.

Day 49

1. How has believing for victory been a struggle for you?

____

____

____

____

2. What might God be trying to teach you in the process?

____

____

____

____

Day 50

Brighter Day

Let me encourage you, not only is this a new day but a brighter day because Jesus is the light of the world. A brighter day has come our way.

> Arise, shine, for your light has come, and the glory of the Lord has risen upon you.
>
> **Isaiah 60:1**

Today's Prayer

I pray for all of my needs to be met.

I pray for the homeless, the lost and the underserved. I pray for the breaking of day in my situations. I thank and pray that the light has come to brighten my path.

Amen.

I decree and declare that

the Light has come into my night.

Day 50

1. How has seeing a brighter day been a struggle for you?

____

____

____

____

2. What might God be trying to teach you in the process?

____

____

____

____

Day 51

Timing Is Everything

God's delay does not mean denial. You can only know the difference if you get before Him and are familiar with His voice. Today I release to God all of my concerns. I pray for a release of miracles, blessings, and answers to what I have put before Him. Don't give up, this time it will work.

> Hope deferred makes the heart sick, but a longing fulfilled is a tree of life.
>
> **Proverbs 13:12**

Today's Prayer

I pray for courage to change my attitudes, behavior and my perspectives through the leading of the Holy Spirit. I pray for clarity in hearing the voice of God. Lord I pray for patience to wait for my change to come.

Amen.

I decree and declare that

I have access and I am no longer denied.

Day 51

1. How has your time with God through prayer been a struggle for you?

____

____

____

____

2. What might God be trying to teach you in the process?

____

____

____

____

Day 52

He is Always with You

Let me encourage you today to know that you are not walking alone.

Trials and tribulations we will have in this life, but God gives us the strength to go through the challenges that are presented to us. Sometimes it feels like we are alone, that there is no one to turn to. Call upon the Lord in those moments of uncertainty.

> I will also walk among you and be your God and you shall be my people.
>
> **Leviticus 26:12**

Today's Prayer

I thank and pray for a closer walk with the Lord. I pray that you are always with me. I pray that I will take accountability for my actions.

Amen.

I decree and declare that

I am not walking alone even when

I feel alone.

Day 52

1. How has knowing God is always with you been a struggle for you?

____

____

____

____

2. What might God be trying to teach you in the process?

____

____

____

____

Day 53

Reshaping

Life has a way of developing us. But if we allow God to have His way, He will show us who we are and the areas that need shaping. He helps us to put down and pick up what is needed to transform us.

> Yet you, Lord, are our Father. We are the clay, you are the potter, we are the work of your hands.
>
> **Isaiah 64:8**

Today's Prayer

I pray that I will submit to the will of God today. I pray for a renewal of my mind and spirit. I pray that I will see through God's lenses for my life. I pray for alignment in areas of my life.

Amen.

I decree and declare that

I am in your hands.

Mold me into what you would have me to be.

Day 53

1. How has reshaping things been a struggle for you?

____

____

____

____

2. What might God be trying to teach you in the process?

____

____

____

____

Day 54

Faithfulness

There are times when we are not as faithful as we would like to be. We procrastinate, we make excuses and even though we meant it at the time that we said it, we fail to honor our own words. Praise be to God that He is always Faithful to His Word. If He said it, believe He will bring it to pass.

> What if some were unfaithful? Will their unfaithfulness nullify God's faithfulness? Not at all! Let God be true, and every human being a liar. As it is written: So that you may be proved right when you speak and prevail when you judge.
>
> **Romans 3:3-4**

Today's Prayer

Heavenly Father, I ask that you teach me how to live a life faithful and pleasing to you. In areas where I have not been faithful, I ask for your forgiveness. I thank you Lord that you are faithful to your Word.

Amen.

I decree and declare that

I want to be faithful to

what You have called me to.

Day 54

1. How has faithfulness been a struggle for you?

____

____

____

____

2. What might God be trying to teach you in the process?

____

____

____

____

Day 55

Praying Together

Could you imagine what it would be like if we came together on one accord in prayer, in our decision making, and our giving? It would spill over into every area of our lives.

> Again, I say to you, that if two of you agree on earth about anything that they may ask, it shall be done for them by My Father who is in heaven.
>
> **Matthew 18:19**

Today's Prayer

I pray for one mind, one spirit, the heartbeat of God. I pray that I would have all things in common and be in synch with my brothers and sisters. I pray for greater sensitivity to the Spirit of God. I pray for unity among those who believe.

Amen.

I decree and declare that
I will agree with what the Word
says about me.

Day 55

1. How has praying with someone been a struggle for you?

____

____

____

____

2. What might God be trying to teach you in the process?

____

____

____

____

Day 56

Works

Do you believe that God is at work in your life? Everything that God made was good. He does not make any junk. You are made in the image of Christ. Being confident of this very thing, that he which hath begun a good work in you will perform it until the day of Jesus Christ.

> For it is God who is at work in you, both to will and to work for His good pleasure.

Philippians 2:13

Today's Prayer

I pray that you are continuously at work in me to bring about your purpose and plan for my life. I pray that you will perfect everything concerning me and when I am feeling overwhelmed that I will remember that I am made in your image and likeness. I pray that as long as I live, I am a work in progress.

Amen.

I decree and declare that
God is at work in me and
He is not finished yet.

Day 56

1. How has believing God is at work in your life been a struggle for you?

____

____

____

____

2. What might God be trying to teach you in the process?

____

____

____

____

Day 57

Escape

How do we escape all the confusion, chaos and evilness that we wake up to everyday? We get into God's presence and meditate on His Word that will carry us through every storm, every fire and every plague and prepare us for what lies ahead.

> In the shelter of your presence, you hide them from all human intrigues; you keep them safe in your dwelling from accusing tongues.
>
> **Psalm 31:20**

Today's Prayer

I pray for God's lovingkindness to draw me into fellowship with Him. I pray that you are keeping me safe and hiding me under the shadow of thy wing. I will speak your Word day and night over my life.

Amen.

I decree and declare that

you will hide me from the enemy.

Day 57

1. How has finding time to escape been a struggle for you?

____

____

____

____

2. What might God be trying to teach you in the process?

____

____

____

____

Day 58

Revelation

There is no expiration date on your faith. Hold fast to your dreams, your promises and the things that God has put in your Spirit. Through the challenges that we face God is causing us to pause and look at what really matters and get to it. Don't let fear paralyze you.

> Write down the revelation and make it plain on tablets, so that a herald may run with it. For the revelation awaits an appointed time, it speaks of the end and it will not prove false. Though it lingers wait for it; it will certainly come and will not delay. It's your time.
>
> **Habakkuk 2:2-3**

Today's Prayer

I pray that I will walk in the revelation that God has given me. I pray for the will of God to be manifest in my life. I pray that my dreams and visions will come to pass.

Amen.

I decree and declare that

I will run with the revelation of the Lord.

Day 58

1. How has seeing revelation from God been a struggle for you?

____

____

____

____

2. What might God be trying to teach you in the process?

____

____

____

____

Day 59

Go for It

I urge you today to take the plunge. What is standing in the way of you giving God 100%? Is it sin, fear, unbelief or weakness? Bring it to Him. He already knows, just lay it down. I do not understand what I do. For what I want to do I do not do, but what I hate I do. God knows your struggle and your help is here.

> Now we who are strong ought to bear the weaknesses of those without strength and not just please ourselves.
>
> **Romans 15:1**

Today's Prayer

I know my weaknesses and ask You for Your strength to overcome them. I pray for total surrender to the things that hinder me. I pray for healing of the whole man, head to toe of all sickness and diseases. Father, I ask that you will raise up Faith Walkers and Prayer Warriors to walk with me through my struggles.

Amen.

I decree and declare that

He that is in me is greater than

he that is in the world.

Day 59

1. How has going for it been a struggle for you?

____

____

____

____

2. What might God be trying to teach you in the process?

____

____

____

____

Devotional Journal

Day 60

Make Room

Let me encourage you today that we need to make room, clear some space, rearrange some things, for what God is going to bring our way. There are some things you might need to get rid of and they can be of use to someone else. Some things you just need to trash. Just let it go! God will give you wisdom to know the difference. God wants to answer you.

> Jabez called out to God of Israel, "If only you would greatly bless me and expand my territory. May your hand be with me! Keep me from harm, so I might not endure pain. God answered his prayer.
>
> **1 Chronicles 4:10**

Today's Prayer

I pray for a move of God in my life that will take me to the next level; the Holy Spirit to speak to me individually and to speak to us collectively. I pray for clarity to know what to remove and when to remove it.

Amen.

I decree and declare that
I move when God says move.

Day 60

1. How has making room for blessings been a struggle for you?

____

____

____

____

2. What might God be trying to teach you in the process?

____

____

____

____

Day 61

Friendship

It's for your good. Don't let it break you it's designed to make you. Before you even get out of bed you are bombarded with the various challenges that await you. I know it can be a lot but Jesus will see you through. He's got your back. This is when we know what we are made of, by how we go through our tests. Sisters and Brothers let's help each other in our tests.

> A man who has friends must be friendly. But there is a friend who sticks closer than a brother.
>
> **Proverbs 18:24**

Today's Prayer

I pray for strength from the Lord to endure what comes my way. I pray and thank you for the friends that you have given me to support, encourage and lift me up. I pray for the building of friendships.

Amen.

I decree and declare that

we can do it together.

Day 61

1. How has friendship been a struggle for you?

____

____

____

____

2. What might God be trying to teach you in the process?

____

____

____

____

Day 62

Submission

Sometimes you have to run for your life to flee from negativity, drama and confusion to obtain what God has for you. I want to encourage you as you go about your day to be careful what you submit to. We must be mindful of the choices that we make; either we submit to the things of God or the things of the Evil one. The Evil one is not coming to you as a devil with a pitch fork, but comes in the form of distraction, deception, procrastination, our children, our jobs, and other ways that pull you from where God is taking you. There is a path that leads to destruction and there is a path that leads to the Blessings of the Lord. Stay on the path that God has ordained for you. If you find yourself on the wrong path cry out to God and He will lead you. Let me encourage you.

> Submit yourselves then, to God. Resist the devil, and he will flee from you.
>
> **James 4:7**

Today's Prayer

I pray that you will choose this day whom you will serve. I pray for a heart of submission to the power of God. Lord teach me how to submit to the Word of God as an act of obedience instead of fear.

Amen.

I decree and declare that
I will submit to what is good and resist
what is evil through the power of the Holy Spirit.

Day 62

1. How has being able to submit been a struggle for you?

____

____

____

____

2. What might God be trying to teach you in the process?

____

____

____

____

Day 63

Influence

Mighty women and men of God I encourage you as you go about your day that the greatest influence upon you will be that of Jesus Christ.

A voice of hope, a voice of promise, a voice of strength and a voice of courage for the times that we are living in this season.

> That your faith should not stand in the wisdom of men, but in the power of God.
>
> **1 Corinthians 2:5**

Today's Prayer

I thank and pray for refueling me for the journey called life. I will read a verse from the Bible, meditate on it and pray to be filled to overflowing capacity with God's Spirit. I pray for the power of God to transform me into who and what I should be. I pray that as the Holy Spirit influences me, I will influence others.

Amen.

I decree and declare that
I am under the influence of the Holy Spirit
as I make decisions that will impact my life.

Day 63

1. How has your influence been a struggle for you?

____

____

____

____

2. What might God be trying to teach you in the process?

____

____

____

____

Day 64

Greatness

Do you know that you have greatness on the inside of you? Everything that you have gone through, every disappointment, every betrayal, every set back was simply preparation for what God is about to do in your life. It was a divine set up. Hallelujah!

If you love God with all of your heart you can experience a fulfillment of this Word.

> A man's gift makes room for him and brings him before the great.
>
> **Proverbs 18:16**

Today's Prayer

Lord open my eyes to see myself and others as you see. I pray for a fresh vision, a fresh revelation of what God is molding and shaping me to be.

Amen.

I decree and declare that

I see me through the eyes of the Spirit.

Day 64

1. How has your greatness been a struggle for you?

____

____

____

____

2. What might God be trying to teach you in the process?

____

____

____

____

Day 65

Push Your Comfort Zone

Let me encourage you today to step out of your comfort zone and pursue what God has set before you. Something is stirring up in you. Test the water and seek God concerning your next step.

What God has called you to do has been on the inside of you and now it is your time to write that song, write that book, design that clothing line, finish your education. Whatever it is, do it now while you have the chance.

> Establish my footsteps in your Word. And do not let any iniquity have dominion over me.
>
> **Psalm 119:133**

Today's Prayer

I pray for courage to step into new territory, new assignments and new revelation without fear and hesitation.

Amen.

I decree and declare that

I will not fear where God is leading me.

Day 65

1. How has pushing back your comfort zone been a struggle for you?

____

____

____

____

2. What might God be trying to teach you in the process?

____

____

____

____

Day 66

New Direction

It has been said, if you keep doing the same thing you will get the same result. Do you want a different outcome in your situation? You can re-write the narrative. What can you do differently? You can change your direction and follow Jesus. Sometimes when you change directions relationships change, environments change, motives change. It's all for your good to bring about the right change in you. Let God do it. Pray and spend some quiet time with the Lord and He will direct you.

> The steps of a man are established by the Lord, And He delights in his way
>
> **Psalm 37:23**

Today's Prayer

I pray for the Holy Spirit to direct my steps and that I may follow Jesus with my whole heart. Lord I pray a spiritual makeover as I step into new direction.

Amen.

I decree and declare that

I am on the right path.

Day 66

1. How has going in a new direction been a struggle for you?

____

____

____

____

2. What might God be trying to teach you in the process?

____

____

____

____

Day 67

Trustworthy

It is very difficult in this season to know who and what to trust. Everyone has an opinion; everyone believes he or she is right.

Let me encourage you today to know that you can trust God.

> But blessed is the one who trusts in the Lord. They will be like a tree planted by the water that sends out its roots by the stream. It does not fear when heat comes; its leaves are always green. It has no worries in a year of drought and never fails to bear fruit.
>
> **Jeremiah 17:7-8**

Today's Prayer

I pray that my faith in Christ will flourish. I pray for healing spiritually, physically and mentally with signs, wonders and miracles to follow all who believe and trust God. Comfort those who mourn the loss of loved ones, and are overwhelmed with grief.

Amen.

I decree and declare that

I will trust what you speak to my spirit.

Day 67

1. How has trust been a struggle for you?

____

____

____

____

2. What might God be trying to teach you in the process?

____

____

____

____

Day 68

Tapping Into Power

Why are some of us hesitant to call on Jesus or we talk to Him after the fact, after we have made a major decision, after things have not worked out? Let's try to call upon Him before the problem, before the breaking of day. There is nothing that we can't talk to Him about.

I want to encourage you to call upon the Name of Jesus because there is Power in that Name. Power to heal, to deliver, to transform, power to believe, power to be saved. God will deliver us from the evil one. He will help us before we enter some situations that we should not go in and bring us out of situations we should not have been in.

> I pray that you will continually experience the immeasurable greatness of God's power made available to you through faith. Then your lives will be advertisement of this immense power as it works through you! This is the mighty power that was released when God raised Christ from the dead and exalted him to the place of highest honor and supreme authority in the heavenly realm.
>
> **Ephesians 1:19-20**

Today's Prayer

I pray that we seek God with our whole heart. I pray for healing the whole man. I pray for healing for all grieving and reliving grief of losses of loved ones. I pray for Signs, Wonders and Miracles to follow all who call upon the Name of Jesus. I pray for exposure to all schemes and strategies of the enemies. Lord I need your resurrection power flowing in my life.

Amen.

I decree and declare that
my life is being transformed by
the power of God.

Day 68

1. How has tapping into your power been a struggle for you?

____

____

____

____

2. What might God be trying to teach you in the process?

____

____

____

____

Day 69

Loved

We serve an awesome God who looks beyond our faults and sees our needs. His love is unconditional and we are made perfect (mature) in Him. Let us learn from Him and not see just the imperfections in others and ourselves but see the Hand of God molding and shaping us to be more like Him. Today, make a decision to love and not criticize, to be patient and remember someone was patient with you. Love is a very powerful weapon. Be encouraged on your journey through life. That is love!

> A new commandment I give to you, that you love one another: just as I have loved you, you also are to love one another. By this all people will know that you are My disciples, if you have love for one another

John 13:34-35

Today's Prayer

I thank God that He loves me unconditionally. I pray for God's love that covers me when I hurt and that the love of God that is in me will touch others. I pray that I will give and receive the love of God wherever I go.

Amen.

I decree and declare that

I will love you unconditionally.

Day 69

1. **How has accepting love been a struggle for you?**

____

____

____

____

2. **What might God be trying to teach you in the process?**

____

____

____

____

Day 70

Prepare

In the south, in the middle of hurricane season people prepare for the storm that is headed in their direction. Preparation begins long before the storm hits. The more intense the storm, the more intense the preparation. We can be prepared through the Word of God to weather the storms of life regardless of how intense it gets. We must daily ask God for forgiveness of our sins, and pray and seek God which prepares us for eternal life.

> Be always on the watch, and pray that you may be able to escape all that is about to happen, and that you may be able to stand before the Son of Man.
>
> **Luke 21:36**

Today's Prayer

I thank and pray for everything that has come my way to prepare me for such a time as this. Lord show me through your Word how to prepare for what lies ahead. I thank you Lord for preparing me for eternal life as I continue to meditate on your Word.

Amen.

I decree and declare that

I am prepared for what comes my way

as I meditate on God's Word.

Day 70

1. How has preparing for what's next been a struggle for you?

____

____

____

____

2. What might God be trying to teach you in the process?

____

____

____

____

Day 71

Higher Ground

I have often heard that our attitude determines our altitude. Do you find that your attitude fluctuates based on what you see, what you hear and what you feel?

As Children of God, we walk in a different realm called faith. We must be influenced by what the Word says over the news, the media and those on Pennsylvania Ave.

> We walk by Faith and not by sight.
>
> **2 Corinthians 5:7**

Today's Prayer

I pray that I will follow the Lord as He leads me. Lord I don't have to know where or how but I will walk as long as you are walking with me. I ask Lord that my faith will not fail me now.

Amen.

I decree and declare that
as I walk in faith, I am going higher
and higher in the Lord.

Day 71

1. How has reaching higher ground in God been a struggle for you?

____

____

____

____

2. What might God be trying to teach you in the process?

____

____

____

____

Day 72

Finding Peace

How do you have peace in the midst of trouble and confusion? In the midst of a health challenge? In the midst of death? We must look at our lives from the Bible's perspective.

> Peace I leave with you; my peace I give to you; I do not give to you as the world gives. Do not let your hearts be troubled; and do not be afraid.
>
> **John 14:27**

Today's Prayer

I thank and pray that peace is my portion and I can have it for the asking. I pray for peace that will see me through all my trials and tribulations. I pray that I will be a peacemaker during times of trouble.

Amen.

I decree and declare that

Satan will not rob me of my peace.

Day 72

1. How has finding peace been a struggle for you?

____

____

____

____

2. What might God be trying to teach you in the process?

____

____

____

____

Day 73

Quenchable Thirst

Are you thirsty, are you experiencing a dry season? Only God can quench the thirst that is deep on the inside of you with living water. Come and drink today.

> As the deer pants for water, so I long for you, O God. I thirst for God, the living God. My prayer for you today is that you allow God to quench your thirst through His Word, through His love and through His peace.

Psalm 42:1

Today's Prayer

I pray Lord that I only thirst for you. I pray that I know that the world can only offer me temporary relief. Lord, I thank you for giving me this living water.

Amen.

I decree and declare that

living water is now flowing in me.

Day 73

1. How has thirsting for more of God been a struggle for you?

____

____

____

____

2. What might God be trying to teach you in the process?

____

____

____

____

Day 74

Trust Renewed Strength

You might have been tossed to the left or the right but you are still standing. I want you to hold on to what God has given you. Even if you feel like throwing in the towel you can't because someone is depending on you. Don't give up, you are so close to what God has promised.

> So do not throw away your confidence; it will be richly rewarded. You need to persevere so that when you have done the will of God, you will receive what he has promised. For, in just a little while, He who is coming will come and will not delay.
>
> **Hebrews 10:35-37**

Today's Prayer

I pray that my strength is renewed. I pray that even in a storm I can see clearly and remain focused. I pray for the Word of God to give me instant replays of what God has done. I will stand on the strength of God's Word in my life.

Amen.

I decree and declare that
I have confidence in what God
has promised me.

Day 74

1. How has renewing your strength in God been a struggle for you?

____

____

____

____

2. What might God be trying to teach you in the process?

____

____

____

____

Day 75

Rescued

Most parents are sensitive to the cry of children, especially the cry of their own. Some answers come quickly and others require patience and are on the way.

> The righteous cry out and He delivers them from all their troubles. The Lord is close to the broken-hearted and saves those who are crushed in spirit.
>
> **Psalm 34:17-18**

Today's Prayer

I thank and pray that God has rescued me from the hand of the enemy and kept me from seen and unseen dangers. I pray that God hears and answers my prayers.

Amen.

I decree and declare that
I will cry out to my Father
when trouble comes.

Day 75

1. How has receiving God's rescue been a struggle for you?

____

____

____

____

2. What might God be trying to teach you in the process?

____

____

____

____

Day 76

Pick Up and Go!

It's time to go from this place. It's time to go from the uncertain to the path of destiny. It's time to turn to our Father for help. My grandmother always taught me "Don't wear your welcome out." Know when it's time to go home.

It's time to pick up what you have put to the side. It's time to face what you did not want to face before. It's time to renew, revive and review areas in your life. If we could do it on our own, we would have done it already. God will bring us back to Him in areas that we have been defeated.

> Restore us to yourself Lord, that we may return; renew our days as of old.

Lamentations 5:21

Today's Prayer

I pray for restoration in every area of my life and the lives of my family. I will hold on to what is good and let go of what is not. I am deleting everything unlike you and I ask for a reset right now. Restore unto me the joy of my salvation.

Amen.

I decree and declare that

restoration has begun.

Day 76

1. How has being able to pick up and go been a struggle for you?

____

____

____

____

2. What might God be trying to teach you in the process?

____

____

____

____

Day 77

Prophecy

When we think of this story we always focus on Mary, the Birth of Jesus and very little is mentioned of Joseph.

Three things Joseph did that I believe will encourage you.

1. He Had a plan based on what he thought and he went to sleep and rested
2. He had a visitation and received clarity
3. Changed his plan and was obedient to God.

We all have thoughts of what we should do, but would we rise up and do what God has asked of us? When we trust God and rest in Him, He will bring clarity to your situation.

> Now the birth of Jesus Christ was on this wise: When his mother Mary had been betrothed to Joseph, before they came together, she was found with child of the Holy Spirit. And Joseph her husband, being a righteous man, and not willing to make her a public example, was

minded to put her away privily.

But when he thought on these things, behold, an angel of the Lord appeared unto him in a dream, saying, Joseph, thou son of David, fear not to take unto thee Mary thy wife: for that which is conceived in her is of the Holy Spirit. And she shall bring forth a son; and thou shalt call his name JESUS; for it is he that shall save his people from their sins.

Now all this is come to pass, that it might be fulfilled which was spoken by the Lord through the prophet, saying, Behold, the virgin shall be with child, and shall bring forth a son, and they shall call his name Immanuel; which is, being interpreted, God with us.

And Joseph arose from his sleep, and did as the angel of the Lord commanded him, and took unto him his wife; and knew her not till she had brought forth a son: and he called his name JESUS

Matthew 1:18-25

Today's Prayer

I believe and receive the prophetic Word of the Lord and all of His promises to manifest in my life with signs, wonders and miracles to follow me all the days of my life.

Amen.

I decree and declare that

I believe the prophecy of Jesus Christ.

Day 77

1. How has receiving the prophecy of God's promises been a struggle for you?

---

2. What might God be trying to teach you in the process?

Day 78

Sow

It is very important in this season that we are mindful of the seeds that we sow. Will you be pleased with what comes up at harvest time? If you sow seeds of love, peace and joy you will reap a harvest based on the seeds you plant. If you sow seeds of doubt, fear and anxiety you will receive a harvest as well. Persevere so that when you have done the will of God you will receive what He has promised. For in just a little while, He who is coming will come and not delay.

> Do not be deceived, God is not mocked; for whatever a man sows, this he will also reap.

Galatians 6:7

Today's Prayer

I pray that I sow seeds, of love, peace and kindness and that they will come back to me. I pray for an overflowing harvest, not just for me, but for all who come in contact with me. Lord I sow my worship and praise to you each and every day.

Amen.

I decree and declare that

the seeds of love that I have sown

will give me a harvest of love.

Day 78

1. How has sowing been a struggle for you?

____

____

____

____

2. What might God be trying to teach you in the process?

____

____

____

____

Day 79

Remember the Good

Believe God for the good things. They will happen for you

> The Lord is good to all; He has compassion on all He has made.
>
> **Psalm 145:9**

Today's Prayer

I pray for the anointing of the Holy Spirit to fall fresh upon me, deliver and set me free from the past that tries to mask the good things God is doing in my life. I pray continued protection from all seen and unseen danger. Help me to remember your grace, mercy and goodness towards me.

Amen.

I decree and declare that

I will not forget what you have done for me.

Day 79

1. How has remembering the good been a struggle for you?

____

____

____

____

2. What might God be trying to teach you in the process?

____

____

____

____

Day 80

Wait

I know you are getting tired of the way things are, frustrated, overwhelmed by changes and challenges in your lives, know that God has a plan for your life. We must hear and pay close attention to what God is saying to us in the midst of the chaos.

Let me encourage you that there is a light at the end of this tunnel. Lord we wait upon you.

> But as for me, I will watch expectantly for the Lord; I will wait for the God of my salvation. My God will hear me.
>
> **Micah 7:7**

Today's Prayer

Lord help me to wait upon you when I feel anxious, afraid and in doubt. I will wait with a spirit of expectation for the things that you will do. I ask for help with my attitude as I wait.

Amen.

I decree and declare that
I will wait until my change comes.

Day 80

1. How has waiting on God been a struggle for you?

____

____

____

____

2. What might God be trying to teach you in the process?

____

____

____

____

Day 81

Precious Gift

Mary, Joseph and the Wise Men anticipated the joy of this special birth. Today we are beneficiaries and join the celebration.

In the midst of our trials and tribulations we can still find joy. This joy won't come through UPS nor will you find it under the tree, but your heart will bubble over with excitement as you focus on Jesus Christ and all that He has done and is doing and will do for us. We have been given a gift, not wrapped in Christmas paper with a red bow, but wrapped in swaddling clothes. Because of His Blood we get to experience this overflowing joy that is birthed in our hearts.

Don't forget about this amazing gift; share it, pass it on knowing that there is none that can top this One.

> For the wages of sin is death, but the gift of God is eternal life in Christ Jesus our Lord.
>
> **Romans 6:23**

Today's Prayer

Lord, I thank you for my precious gift that I will always treasure. I will show my appreciation by sharing with as many as I can. I will celebrate and enjoy all that the Father has given to me. I pray that we will glorify God like Mary did and know that the Favor of God is with all of us.

Amen.

I decree and declare that

I will celebrate the gift of life

that gave me eternal life.

Day 81

1. How has receiving the gift been a struggle for you?

____

____

____

____

2. What might God be trying to teach you in the process?

____

____

____

____

Devotional Journal

Day 82

Celebrate

I would like to encourage you as you continue in this celebration to be the best Ambassador for Christ that you can be. You are the Church and might be the only Bible that will be read. The world is looking for answers, people are looking for hope, and we got the goods.

> But in your hearts honor Christ the Lord as Holy, always being prepared to make a defense to anyone who asks you for a reason for the hope that is in you; yet do it with gentleness and respect.
>
> **1 Peter 3:15**

Today's Prayer

My prayer is that I honor and celebrate God in all that I do. I thank Him for the good and the not so good. I will celebrate the King of Kings and the Lord of Lords. I will celebrate others and will honor the God in them. I pray for revelation of what you are carrying in this season. I pray that we will complete the assignment that our Heavenly Father has given us.

Amen.

I decree and declare that

I will celebrate the Christ in you.

Day 82

1. How has celebration been a struggle for you?

2. What might God be trying to teach you in the process?

Day 83

Loose Ends

As I began to meditate this morning I could hear in my spirit, "Tie up any loose ends before going into the next season, next relationship, next assignment, next year. Honor your word. If you made any commitments, honor them, if you made any vows, honor them. If you can't honor them acknowledge them and the Grace of God will be with you.

If God has spoken to you to forgive, honor it, it's time to let it go. Whatever God has instructed you to do, honor it. We Honor God and we honor one another. That is love.

Be encouraged.

> But whoever keeps his word, truly the love of God is perfected; hereby know we are in Him.
>
> **1 John 2:5**

Today's Prayer

Lord I am listening and I hear Your voice and I will honor You in all that I do. I will follow all of Your instructions and obey Your Word. I pray for healing in body, mind and spirit.

Amen.

I decree and declare that

we are created to bring Honor to God.

Day 83

1. How have loose ends been a struggle for you?

____

____

____

____

2. What might God be trying to teach you in the process?

____

____

____

____

Day 84

Transformed

Transformation is at work in our members because it is an ongoing process in the life of a believer. The Word of God transforms our minds and our hearts and brings us into unity with the Father and each other. I encourage you to keep your eyes fixed on Jesus. He is the real transformer; He is the One who connects it all together. He is our heart fixer and mind regulator.

> And do not be conformed to this world, but be transformed by the renewing of your mind, so that you may prove what the will of God is, that which is good and acceptable and perfect.
>
> **Romans 12:2**

Today's Prayer

My prayer for you today is that you be renewed in your heart and mind. I pray that Healing and deliverance will touch you and your families today. I pray for signs, wonders and miracles to follow all who believe.

Amen.

I decree and declare that

I am transforming because

God is doing a work in me.

Day 84

1. How has transformation been a struggle for you?

____

____

____

____

2. What might God be trying to teach you in the process?

____

____

____

____

Day 85

Excess

Make sure that you are not carrying excess baggage into new seasons, new relationships and new assignments. Let's start by leaving all negativity behind. Fear is not going with me, nor doubt or I can't. We will carry faith, peace and joy to the next level. I know that we will always have trials and tribulations but make sure we don't pick up what we have put down.

It is time to let go of all the weight that you have been carrying. Just drop it. I want to encourage you to raise your expectations. Raise your service to God and each other. Let this year be a year of accelerated Fellowship with the Father, and more time in Worship, His Word, and Prayer.

My prayer for you today is that we work together as one body and do what God has assigned us to do.

> Therefore since we are surrounded by such a great cloud of witnesses, let us throw off everything that hinders and the sin that so easily entangles. And let us run with perseverance the race marked out for us.
>
> **Hebrews 12:1**

Today's Prayer

Lord, I need You to help me with my excess and through the Holy Spirit remove it from the areas of my life that you shine the light upon. I will not stay in the past but I will move forward shedding former hurt, pain and disappointments.

Amen.

I decree and declare that
I only take what I need for my journey.

Day 85

1. **How has excess in your life been a struggle for you?**

---

2. **What might God be trying to teach you in the process?**

Day 86

Step Up

I believe that God has called us to step up; to intensify in the things of God. Since we are in different places, we have different areas that God is requiring us to step up into. It may be His Presence, Worship, Prayer, Fasting, or reading the Word. We will see a new improved version of ourselves if we are obedient to God's instructions. This is a new day, full of possibility, promise and purpose. We need new instructions, because we have shifted.

> Be encouraged from the Word of the Lord, "No one sews a patch of un-shrunk cloth on an old garment, for the patch will pull away from the garment, making the tear worse. Neither do people pour new wine into old wineskins. If they do the skins will burst, the wine will run out and the wineskins will be ruined. No, they pour new wine into new wineskins, and both are preserved.
>
> **Matthew 9:16-17**

Today's Prayer

I will seek You with my whole heart and embrace the newness of life live out my journey. Help me Lord to always seek You for Your will in my life. I pray when difficulties come my way, I will call on Your Name to pour out your Anointing upon me.

Amen.

I decree and declare that

I want to experience something new in God.

Day 86

1. How has stepping up your walk been a struggle for you?

____

____

____

____

2. What might God be trying to teach you in the process?

____

____

____

____

Day 87

Confidence

I am more confident than ever that God will take care of us in these difficult days. What road will you travel today?

Travel that leads to peace, or travel that leads to destruction? My prayer for you today is that you change lanes if you have to. I pray that you follow God.

> Enter through the narrow gate. For wide is the gate and broad is the road that leads to destruction, and many enter through it. But small is the gate and narrow the road that leads to life, and only a few find it.

Matthew 7:13-14

Today's Prayer

I need Your Spirit as I travel these difficult roads ahead of me. Roads of uncertainty, roads of unfamiliarity, roads of racism, poverty and fear. I am confident that I am not traveling them alone.

Amen.

I decree and declare that

I am not traveling alone.

Day 87

1. How has your confidence level been a struggle for you?

____

____

____

____

2. What might God be trying to teach you in the process?

____

____

____

____

Day 88

Weapon of Praise

We thank God that He didn't hold back this day and we are still here. Let everything that has breath Praise the Lord. We have a tendency to praise God when things are going well, kids are behaving, money in the bank. I dare you to praise Him in the midst of chaos and confusion, or when you have received a negative report. Do you know that praise is a weapon against the enemy? It has been said that when the praises go up the blessings come down.

> Through Jesus, therefore let us continually offer to God a sacrifice of Praise- the fruit of lips that openly profess his name.

Hebrews 13:15

Today's Prayer

I praise God with every breath in my body. I will give him praise through the darkest and the brightest of times. I know that my praise is a weapon against the enemy and I will use it to stop the enemy in his tracks.

Amen.

I decree and declare that

I am a Praiser and my Worship is authentic.

Day 88

1. How has using your weapons of praise been a struggle for you?

____

____

____

____

2. What might God be trying to teach you in the process?

____

____

____

____

Day 89

Favor

The Favor of God will exceed your expectations and cause others to show favor to you. Take a moment and shower God with your Praise. Expect the extraordinary! Our Father does amazing things for us because He loves us and it is His good pleasure. We can't earn it nor do we deserve it.

> May the favor of the Lord our God rest on us; establish the work of our hands for us - yes establish the work of our hands.

Psalm 90:17

Today's Prayer

My prayer for you today is that you decree the Word over you. Remember me Lord when you show favor to your people, help me when you save them. (Psalm 106:4)

I pray that the favor of God is upon my life and goes before me in all that I endeavor.

Amen.

I decree and declare that
I have found favor with God.

Day 89

1. How has receiving God's favor been a struggle for you?

____

____

____

____

2. What might God be trying to teach you in the process?

____

____

____

____

Day 90

He is with You Always

For some of us have been blessed with a season full of love, peace and joy. For others a time of loss of loved ones, lack of peace, health concerns, and just unexpected situations and fear of the unknown. Or maybe you have had a little bit of both.

I am here to let you know that God is moving, keep watching. Change is coming, your miracle is on the way and your breakthrough is breaking through! Whatever side of the spectrum that you find yourself God is there. He is with you on the mountain top and He is with you in the valley.

> Let us therefore draw near with boldness unto the throne of grace, that we may receive mercy, and may find grace to help us in time of need. For we have not a high priest that cannot be touched with the feeling of our infirmities; but one that hath been in all points tempted like as we are, yet without sin.
>
> **Hebrews 4:15-16**

Today's Prayer

I pray that because of Jesus I can bring everything to the Lord in prayer. I am grateful that He knows my name and I know to call on His name.

Amen.

I decree and declare that

my life has been touched by God

and it will never be the same.

Day 90

1. How has knowing you are not alone been a struggle for you?

____

____

____

____

2. What might God be trying to teach you in the process?

____

____

____

____

Devotional Journal

MY PRAYER FOR THE NATIONS

I THANK AND PRAY FOR HEALING, DELIVERANCE AND RESTORATION IN EVERY AREA OF OUR LIFE AND THE LIVES OF OUR FAMILIES AND FRIENDS WITH SIGNS, WONDERS AND MIRACLES TO FOLLOW ALL WHO BELIEVE.

I THANK AND PRAY FOR THE BLOOD OF JESUS COVERING AND PROTECTING US FROM THE EVIL ONE AND KEEPING US SAFE DURING THIS SEASON IN OUR LIVES. I PRAY FOR COMFORT AND PEACE FOR ALL WHO MOURN THE LOSS OF LOVED ONES. I PRAY FOR OUR LEADERSHIP AND ASK FOR GOD'S SUPERNATURAL TOUCH UPON ALL. I PRAY AND THANK GOD FOR MEN AND WOMEN OF FAITH AS THEY PRAY AND INTERCEDE FOR OUR WORLD. I ASK THAT WE PRAY ONE FOR ANOTHER AND THAT GOD'S WILL BE DONE ON EARTH. I PRAY

THAT WE EXPERIENCE GOD'S LOVE IN A POWERFUL WAY. I THANK AND PRAY FOR BLESSINGS OF GOD TO REST ON EACH OF US.

If you have never accepted Jesus Christ as your Lord and Savior, please repeat these words:

> *Romans 10:9-10 says, "If you declare with your mouth, Jesus is Lord and believe in your heart that God raised Him from the dead, you will be saved. For it is with your heart that you believe and are justified, and it is with your mouth that you profess your faith and are saved."*
>
> *Father, I ask that you would forgive me of my sins and come in my heart and be my Lord and Savior.*

If you have made this step Congratulations! This is the beginning of the rest of your life. God will put people in your path to help you with the next steps.

REV. DR. PAMELA D. HAILEY-GILLARD

Made in the USA
Coppell, TX
24 April 2022